PEAK DISTRICT
FROM ABOVE

TOP LEFT: Maze at Chatsworth, TOP RIGHT: Fields at Tideswell, ABOVE: Chatsworth House, BOTTOM LEFT: Haddon Hall, BOTTOM RIGHT: Buxton.

PHOTOGRAPHS BY
JASON HAWKES
TEXT BY ADELE McCONNEL

MYRIAD BOOKS LIMITED

CHATSWORTH HOUSE AND GARDENS

THE HISTORY OF THE HOME of the Duke and Duchess of Devonshire dates back to 1549, when Sir William Cavendish bought the estate from the Agard family and began building the original Chatsworth House. After his death in 1557, his widow, Bess of Hardwick, oversaw the completion of a three-storey Elizabethan structure that enclosed a central courtyard. At the end of the 17th century, the first Duke of Devonshire set about rebuilding the house and developing the formal gardens, and 70 years later the grounds changed again when Capability Brown was engaged to landscape the vast park.

The north wing of the house was added by the 6th Duke, by all accounts an extravagant bachelor, in the 1820s. He also employed Joseph Paxton, the designer of London's Crystal Palace, to work on the gardens and together they were responsible for installing the Emperor Fountain, once the world's highest gravity-fed jet.

After these alterations, little changed until after the Second World War, when debts put severe financial restraints on the family. An agreement was reached with the government to open the house to the general public, and a maze made of 1,209 yew trees was planted in 1962, in the middle section of the Old Conservatory Garden. Today, many of the 175 rooms have been converted to flats, offices and storage areas and Chatsworth is run by a charitable trust.

 ## RIBER CASTLE (LEFT)

ALSO KNOWN AS SMEDLEY'S FOLLY, Riber Castle can be seen from almost every street in Matlock.
It was designed by John Smedley in the 1860s as a family home, and as a guest house for some of the more
distinguished visitors to the Hydro. Built of large gritstone blocks, the building was not to everyone's taste.
John Summerson, one of Britain's foremost architectural writers, thought he had never seen a building 'so lacking
in grace'. Riber cost Smedley £60,000 to build, but by the time the British Fauna Reserve bought it from the
council in 1963, it had fallen into such disrepair that the price was a mere £500. Today, the folly stands in ruins
although a new owner has recently acquired the castle and there are plans to develop it for residential use.

CRICH CLIFF QUARRY (ABOVE)

GEORGE STEPHENSON, whose portrait appears on the reverse of £5 notes, originally owned the
Crich Cliff Quarry. In 1841 he began to transport limestone from the quarry site to Ambergate to be used for
burning and for conversion into lime for agriculture. Nowadays the trams that travel along the quarry floor are
for tourists and the National Tramway museum, started in 1959, houses around 50 trams
of which about a third are in working order.
Above the quarry, on top of the cliff, is a war memorial in the form of a lighthouse tower for the
Sherwood Foresters (Nottingham and Derbyshire regiment). On the first Sunday of every July there is
a ceremony to commemorate all those who saw active service and made the ultimate sacrifice.

MATLOCK (ABOVE) AND **MATLOCK BATH** (RIGHT)

JUST OUTSIDE the Peak District National Park, situated at a sharp bend in the River Derwent, lies the
county town of Derbyshire: Matlock. Although the Romans are thought to have mined lead here, it was the
development as a spa that brought notoriety when thermal springs were discovered in 1698.
In the early 19th century, John Smedley built a vast hydro on the steep hill to the north of the river crossing which
continued to attract visitors. The arrival of the Midland Railway in 1865 brought further prosperity
in the shape of day trippers from the Derby-Nottingham area.
Enclosed by the limestone cliffs of the gorge, Matlock Bath simultaneously developed tourist attractions
to ensure a steady stream of visitors. Today these include show caverns, cable railways, petrifying wells
and pleasure gardens.

LADYBOWER RESERVOIR

KNOWN COLLECTIVELY AS the "Peakland Lake District", Ladybower reservoir is the largest of a chain
of three massive reservoirs with the other two, Howden and Derwent, lying further up the valley.
It was completed in 1945 and provides drinking water for the north and east Midlands. Two villages, Derwent
and Ashopton, were sacrificed to the construction of the reservoir and many buildings were submerged.
Amongst those that lie below the waters are a parish church, the spire of which could be seen
while the water level was low, an ancient farm, and Derwent Hall, a property of the Duke of Norfolk
dating back to 1672.

CHESTERFIELD

CHESTERFIELD **IS BEST-KNOWN** for its church 'St Marys and All Saints Parish
Church', not because it is the largest church in Derbyshire but because of its
infamous 238-foot Crooked Spire. The spire not only leans approximately nine and
a half feet away from the true centre, but is also twisted. As an important local
landmark, the spire has been used as a symbol to represent many
local organisations and the town uses the motto 'Aspire' in its honour.
The church faced destruction in 1961 when a fire broke out in the north transept,
and it took firemen two hours to get the blaze under control.
The cost of the damage was around £30,000.
Legends abound about how the spire became crooked. One story tells of how a
blacksmith drove a nail into the Devil's foot when shoeing him. Howling with rage
the Devil took flight and lashed out in anger over Chesterfield, catching the spire
and twisting it out of shape. Another story tells of the rumour that a virgin was
getting married at the church, and the spire, having never seen a virgin bride, leaned
over to have a closer look. Should the event ever happen again, the spire will think
it commonplace and straighten up. There are of course more mundane
explanations such as the lack of cross-bracing, resulting in the spire being unable to
fully support the heavy lead tiles (32 tons in total), or the use of unseasoned timber
in its construction, which may have warped in warm weather. Either of these may
have been down to the Black Death which swept the area in 1349 – around the
same time that the spire was built. If the plague killed skilled workers,
those with less experience would have been left to finish the work.

LIMESTONE GORGES AND THE **RIVER WYE** (ABOVE, LEFT AND RIGHT)

THE SCENERY HERE IS BREATHTAKING. There are huge limestone gorges created by the River Wye. Places such as Water-cum-Jolly, a magnificent river gorge with fine limestone cliffs attract many rock-climbers, walkers and fishermen. Also Ravensdale, a fine gorge-like limestone dale with numerous crags and the remains of several lead mines. Most of this dale is a National Nature Reserve renowned for its range of rare fauna and flora.

MONSAL VIADUCT (RIGHT)

BUILT IN 1863 AS PART OF the Midland Line, Monsal Viaduct is today listed as being of both architectural and historic interest. However, when the route was first proposed it caused an outcry as it was seen as the needless desecration of the countryside. The eminent writer and critic John Ruskin was particularly vociferous on the subject, cursing the loss of a valley *'once upon a time divine as the Vale of Tempe; you might have seen the Gods there morning and evening – Apollo and all the sweet Muses of the light….'.*

Luckily, public opinion is now more positive about the Victorian engineering that has become an integral part of the Monsal Dale scenery and plans are being developed to restore the railway line across the viaduct, ultimately linking Matlock to Buxton.

BAKEWELL (LEFT)

BUILT ON THE WEST BANK of the River Wye where it was fordable, Bakewell has probably been occupied since Roman times. The Doomsday Book entry calls the town 'Badequella', meaning Bath-well, and the name is said to derive from the warm springs in the area. In the 1700s, the Duke of Rutland tried to develop a spa here that would rival Buxton springs, but he failed and today only Bath Gardens stands as a reminder of the venture. However, the town gamed fame with the advent of the almond-flavoured Bakewell tart, said to be invented here accidentally in 1860 when a cook botched a recipe for strawberry tart.

HADDON HALL (ABOVE)

HAILED AS THE FINEST EXAMPLE of a medieval manor house currently in existence in England, Haddon Hall lies two miles south of Bakewell alongside the River Wye. The hall is one of the seats of the Dukes of Rutland, but was used very little in the 18th and 19th centuries when the Devonshires built nearby Chatsworth House. It therefore escaped Georgian and Victorian additions and remained almost unaltered from the end of the 16th century until the 1920s when the 9th Duke of Rutland began restoration. The Hall was used as the location for Mr Rochester's Thornfield in Franco Zeffirelli's production of Jane Eyre.

TIDESWELL (ABOVE)

EVIDENCE OF NEOLITHIC REMAINS have been found in the area, making
Tideswell one of the most ancient settlements in the central Peak District. Some
people believe the village takes its name from a 7th century Saxon chief called 'Tidi',
whereas others attribute the name to the Tiding Well on Manchester Road.
Due to a natural syphon in the rock, the well did actually ebb and flow until the end
of the 18th century. The village was a major lead-mining centre from the 14th century
until the 19th century and the local miners were well known for their strength and
were well regarded by the military authorities. When a group of miners were
paraded before him in London, King George III is reported to have exclaimed, *'I don't
know what effect these men will have on the enemy, but good God they frighten me'*.

BUXTON (RIGHT)

THE NAME ON MILLIONS OF mineral water bottle labels, Buxton has been
exploited for its springs since 79AD. The Romans set up camp here when they
discovered a spring which produced 1,500 gallons of pure water every hour
at a constant temperature of 28°C. The Duke of Devonshire envisaged Buxton
as the northern alternative to Bath and took steps to establish the town as such,
but his plan was ultimately thwarted by the unfavourable climate.
However, the thermal baths didn't close until 1972 and the locals can still be
seen filling their water bottles at St Ann's Well.

ASHFORD IN THE WATER

SITUATED ON THE RIVER WYE, one and a half miles north west of Bakewell, is Ashford in the
Water. There is a custom here called 'Well Dressing'. As homage to the abundance of water,
six wells are dressed by layering petals, leaves and other natural objects such as sage and straw into
a bed of clay. Some sources attribute the practice to the period of the Black Death in 1348-49,
when around a third of the population of England died of the disease while others were untouched.
Most people attributed this to their clean water supply and gave thanks by 'dressing' the village wells.
However, it is likely that the practice goes back much further than this – perhaps to pagan times – and
the fact that many well dressings have a 'well queen' hint at fertility rites. At Ashford in the Water,
the ancient custom fell into disuse until Ida Thorpe revived it around 40 years ago. Now, during
well-dressing week, the church can expect to receive around 12,000 visitors.

WALKERS ALONG THE RIDGE
IN PEAK NATIONAL PARK (LEFT)

THIS RIDGE NEAR CASTLETON provides walkers with truly
spectacular views across the National Park. The park itself was the first
to be set up in Britain in 1951.

LOOKING ALONG CLIFFS
AT CURBAR EDGE (ABOVE)

SPECTACULAR VIEWS ARE to be had from the top of Curbar
Edge, across the Derwent valley to Eyam, Stoney Middleton, Calver,
Curbar and Baslow, a gritstone escarpment which is a famous point
for climbers and walkers.

STONEY MIDDLETON (ABOVE)

STONEY **MIDDLETON IS A VILLAGE** at the foot of Middleton Dale, seen in the background of this image, a spectacular cliff-lined valley. Once again the area surrounding the village is loved by serious climbers for excellent and difficult routes.

LONGNOR (RIGHT)

LONGNOR WAS EXCLUDED from the Doomsday Book, despite the belief that William the Conqueror visited the area in 1070 to quell revolts on the moorlands. Historians first found mention of the village in the 13th century, and it is known that the 20 homes that existed here in 1563 had increased to 39 by the end of the 17th century. However, the area's height of prosperity came in the 1850s, when the population swelled to 561 and it was referred to as a market town.

Lately Longnor, meaning 'long ridge', has gained notoriety as the location of the popular ITV drama series 'Peak Practice' and aficionados will easily be able to identify various landmarks from the programme around the village.

RAMSHAW ROCKS (LEFT)

THE ROACHES AND RAMSHAW ROCKS are dramatic, jagged ridges with breathtaking views, and some of the best grit stone rock climbing in the country. To the east is the White Peak, with its steep dales, dry stone walls and sweeping panoramas – including the deep, twisting gorge of the Manifold Valley, one of the County's outstanding beauty spots.

CURBAR EDGE (BELOW)

CHROME HILL

THE SPECTACULAR CHROME HILL, along with
nearby Parkhouse Hill, are favourite walking routes
due to the panoramic view that they offer.

These hills, notably Chrome Hill and Parkhouse Hill,
are the remains of coral reefs which once made up
the edge of the shallow lagoon in which the
limestone rocks were laid down in the early
Carboniferous era, 340 million years ago.
They are among the most spectacular sights
of the area. This short walk starts from the
charming little hamlet of Hollinsclough on the
gritstone of the Staffordshire side of the river and
crosses to the Derbyshire side to make
a traverse of the spectacular ridge of Chrome Hill
before returning.

LIMESTONE GORGES AND THE RIVER WYE

CRESSBROOK IS A TYPICAL VILLAGE in this area lying just past the meandering River Wye, at the head of Monsal Dale. It used to be a mill village on the River Wye, though some of the houses in and around the village are lead miners' cottages. The mill built by Sir Richard Arkwright in 1785 is still the largest building in the village and although it used to be in ruins it is now in the process of being restored.

BOLSOVER CASTLE (LEFT)

NOT THAT MUCH IS KNOWN about the original castle at Bolsover, except that it was built by the Peverel family in the 12th century and became Crown property in 1155 when the third William Peverel fled into exile. A stone keep was built around 1173, surrounded by a curtain wall which was eventually breached in 1216 during the reign of King John. Surviving fragments of this curtain wall were later incorporated in a wall walk that can be seen in the castle garden.

Much of what can be seen today dates back to the 17th century. The castle is now the subject of the *Bolsover Castle Development Project*, a scheme instigated by English Heritage and financed by grants totalling £3m.

ALTON TOWERS (ABOVE)

JUST SOUTH of the Peak district, what is now known as Alton Towers started life as a summer estate for the Earl of Shrewsbury and his family and was known as Alveton Lodge. It changed hands many times over the years and was subject to periods of intense neglect – not least when the post-second world war shortages of copper and lead meant that the interior of the house was stripped. However, the future began to look brighter for the property when John Broome decided to turn the 500-acre site into a family leisure park in the 1980s. Today the park is visited by thousands of people a year and is home to thrilling rides such as the Corkscrew rollercoaster and the Oblivion ride, which drops down vertically.

BOLSOVER CASTLE (ABOVE)

First Published in 2002 by Myriad Books Limited,
35 Bishopsthorpe Road, London SE26

Photographs Copyright Jason Hawkes
Text Copyright Adele McConnel

Jason Hawkes has asserted his right under the
Copyright, Designs and Patents Act, 1998, to be
identified as the author of this work.

ISBN 1 904154 31 X

Designed by David Fordham
Printed in China